WARSHIPS ILLUSTRATED No 5

1. *Repulse* (named, like her sister-boats, after a class of early twentieth century battleships) was the second of the Polaris boats, or 'bomber boats' as their crews call them. On the bridge is the Captain, First Lieutenant, Navigator and three other officers. The round plate between the control planes is the forward escape hatch; aft of this is the Graseby sonar antenna. (RN/HMS *Neptune*)

⚓ WARSHIPS ILLUSTRATED No 5

Nuclear Powered Submarines

PAUL BEAVER

ARMS AND ARMOUR PRESS

London   New York   Sydney

Introduction

Published in 1986 by Arms & Armour Press Ltd.,
2–6 Hampstead High Street, London NW3 1QQ.

Distributed in the United States by Sterling
Publishing Co. Inc., 2 Park Avenue, New York,
N.Y.10016.

British Library Cataloguing in Publication Data:
Beaver, Paul
Nuclear-powered submarines.—(Warships
illustrated; 5)
1. Nuclear submarines—History
I. Title   II. Series
623.8′2574′0904   VM317

ISBN 0-85368-733-1

Editing, design and artwork by Roger Chesneau.
Typesetting by Typesetters (Birmingham) Ltd.
Printed and bound in Italy
by GEA/GEP in association with
Keats European Ltd., London.

Just as the aircraft carrier superseded the battleship in the Second World War, so the nuclear-powered submarine has overtaken the carrier as the Cold War's capital ship. The true submarine, able to keep submerged for as long as the food lasts (and for as long as the crew can psychologically stand it), is today the master of the seas. Yet it has been a relatively short rise to fame: although the Germans had begun to develop submarines capable of very long patrols into the deep Atlantic during the latter stages of the Second World War, it was not until the nuclear reactor had been perfected in the 1960s that the submarine could be expected to realise its true potential.

There is still much debate about the 'nuclear submarine question', and there are many ill-informed observers. Too many people believe that a nuclear submarine is one with nuclear weapons aboard. Whilst this can be so, the majority of the world's three hundred and seventy or so nuclear-powered submarines (in service, building, or in reserve) are conventionally armed in peacetime, and designated SSN. The boats carrying the nuclear weapons are the ballistic missile submarines (SSBN) and, in the case of the Soviet Navy, the cruise missile carriers (SSGN), although, admittedly, the torpedo 'technology lag' of the Soviets could mean that small nuclear devices tip their torpedoes to give greater lethality.

Over the next few years, the navies of the world will place more emphasis on the quietness of their boats, on the capabilities of their passive sonars (for long-range undetected detection) and on their ability to carry, aim and fire stand-off weapons like Sub-Harpoon. There is no doubt that the new capital ships are here to stay, but the 'club' to which currently five nations belong – China (People's Republic), France, the United Kingdom, the USA and the USSR – will not easily find new members, so costly is the construction of the nuclear-powered, deep-diving submarine and so important is it to have crews with exceptional training.

Paul Beaver

◀2
2. The French Navy uses a diesel-electric submarine, *Gymnote*, for trials associated with the SNLE programme, and in 1984 a scale model of the M-4 missile was loaded into *Gymnote*'s tubes to confirm its handling characteristics. The trials took place in the Ile Longue submarine facilities at the Brest naval base in Brittany. (SNIAS)

▲3 ▼4

5▲

3, 4. In 1974 the French government decided to invest many millions of francs in the development of nuclear-powered fleet-type submarines ('SNA' in French terminology). The first of the class was ordered in that year, was launched in 1979 and entered service in 1983 as *Rubis*. She is equipped with sonar and electronics gear similar to that carried aboard the latest French conventional submarines, her armament being up to fourteen heavyweight torpedoes and/or mines, plus the new SM.39 submarine-launched Exocet (photograph 4), which was test-fired successfully in May 1985. The view of *Rubis* shows the passive ranging sonar and fin-top radio equipment. Note the position of the hydroplanes: because of their position on the fin they cannot be effective during diving and surfacing. It is intended to have at least six of the type in service by 1990. (ECPA/Aérospatiale)

5. *Rubis* makes a dive, her attack periscope raised and her fin hydroplanes tilted down (but unable to gain contact with the water). This photograph was probably taken during the submarine's preliminary cruise in the Atlantic in 1982, the boat having been built at Cherbourg Naval Dockyard. In operational use, she would probably not carry the pennant number nor the name on the fin. (ECPA)

6. France's policy of independence in matters of defence led to the establishment of the *Force de Dissuasion*, thence to the building of the first nuclear-powered ballistic missile submarines for the French Navy in the 1960s. *Le Foudroyant* was launched at Cherbourg in December 1971 and became operational in June 1974. By 1980 she had been joined by four sister-ships, giving the French a more flexible operational arrangement than the Royal Navy, which has only four boats. A new class of SNLE (French naval terminology for SSBN) has been ordered, with two boats due to be commissioned by 1990.

6▼

7. Using *Gymnote* as the test vehicle, the M-4 was first launched in 1980, to prove the missile concept in time for its introduction into service in *L'Inflexible* in 1985. The test was carried out in the Bay of Biscay, adjacent to the *Centre d'Essais des Landes*, near Biscarrosse. In addition to having SLBMs, the SNLEs will be armed with SM.39 Exocet and have at least six 21in (53cm) torpedo tubes for self-defence and limited offensive action. (CET)

8. In the late 1950s the Royal Navy made the decision to enter the nuclear-powered submarine business in earnest with the development of a prototype fleet-type submarine to track, engage and destroy enemy submarines. Originally it was hoped that this craft, to be called *Dreadnought*, would be propelled by a British-designed nuclear reactor, but in 1959 it was announced that American equipment would be purchased. *Dreadnought* was laid down on 12 June 1959, was launched the following October and entered RN service in 1963. She was paid off in 1982. (RN/HMS *Neptune*)

9. In 1966 *Valiant* became the Royal Navy's second nuclear-powered attack submarine (SSN) and the first to be powered by a British reactor; she is seen here negotiating the Faslane narrows as she heads for the open sea. The boat's bridge (atop the fin) is manned by the Captain (usually a Commander RN), the First Lieutenant and the Navigator; on the casing, immediately forward of the sonar mast, is the Casing Officer, responsible for mooring lines and other related activities. (RN/HMS *Neptune*)

▲7 ▼8

9▶

10. *Valiant* underway in the North Atlantic. The design of the boat is broadly similar to that of *Dreadnought* but is scaled up in certain areas to reflect the experience of operating the first SSN. In this view, the Barr & Stroud search periscope has been raised and the pennant number, S102, is just visible on the fin. British submarines no longer wear pennant numbers and this photograph must have been taken between the time the decision was made to remove the numbers and the boat's next docking, where it would have been completely obliterated. (RN/PRB3171/9)

11. After *Valiant* came *Warspite*, another famous battleship name from earlier this century. Like most of Britain's nuclear-powered attack submarines, *Warspite* was built by Vickers at Barrow-in-Furness; she is seen here leaving Faslane naval base. The casing party appears to be stowing the mooring wires and the nuclear safety boat is in attendance. Above the fin, the radio mast and search periscopes have been extended. (RN/HMS *Neptune*)

10▲   11▼

▲12

12. Modern naval tactics require the complete integration of submarines with surface combat ships and anti-submarine helicopters. The helicopter can often act as a liaison vehicle: here *Valiant* awaits the delivery of extra personnel from a Sea King helicopter from Prestwick. These helicopters also support the nuclear-powered ballistic missile-carrying boats based at Faslane and take the opportunity of operating with friendly SSNs whenever the occasion arises. (RN/HMS *Gannet*)

13. In 1965 the British government announced its intention of building three 'Improved *Valiant*' Class SSNs at a cost of about £30 million each. The first of these three new boats was named *Churchill*, after the British wartime leader and former First Lord of the Admiralty, was launched in 1967 and was completed four years later. Compared to the first two *Valiants*, the boat has an improved internal layout and better sonar equipment. In 1979–81 *Churchill* was the trials boat for the Sub-Harpoon anti-ship missile which is now in fleet service with the Submarine Flotilla. (RN/HMS *Neptune*)

▼13

14, 15. In May 1983 *Churchill* departed from the Royal Naval Dockyard at Chatham following a major refit there; she was the last nuclear-powered submarine to use the yard before it closed later that year. Supported by several harbour tugs of the Royal Maritime Auxiliary Service, *Churchill* was fed through the series of lock gates into the River Medway and so to the Thames Estuary for sea trials. Only two dockyards now have SSN repair facilities – Rosyth in Scotland, where the SSBNs are also refitted, and HM Dockyard at Plymouth. (RN/HMS *Pembroke*)

14▲

15▼

16. The nuclear-powered attack submarine is not really at home on the surface of the sea: being a true submarine, it is designed and built to operate underwater. The large control planes, at either end of the cigar-shaped hull, together with the large rudder, control the boat in rather the same way as an aircraft flies through the air. In confined waters, where surface passage is necessary, the SSN looks a little ungainly and can prove uncomfortable for the ship's company inside; this view of *Conqueror* certainly gives that impression. (RN/HMS *Neptune*)

17. Pushing the submarine's characteristic bow wave in front, *Courageous*, the third of the 'Improved *Valiant*' Class SSNs, moves down from *Neptune*, the Faslane naval establishment, towards the Clyde. At nearly 5,000 tons dived, *Courageous* is a large, heavy boat to manoeuvre in confined waters, and each passage to and from Faslane is carefully monitored. Above the fin, the radio and search periscope masts have been raised, the former to maintain contact with operations control at *Neptune* and the latter as an aid to navigation in confined waters. (RN/HMS *Neptune*)

18. When running on the surface, *Courageous* raises her navigation and search radar (similar to that fitted in many surface warships) as well as her radio mast (aft), attack periscope and larger search periscope. On the forward casing are the domes of two sonar sets; the other sonar arrays are mounted in the hull and not visible in this view. (RN/HMS *Excellent*)

19. The surface navy has always been rather curious about the nuclear-powered submarine and the 'strange' world of the submariner. This photograph of *Courageous* undertaking a familiarization cruise for naval officers shows the rather cramped conditions atop the fin. The fin is what many people still call the 'conning tower', but the latter is a small dome within the submarine's pressure hull. The fin is almost totally free-flooding apart from the series of hatches for the conning tower. (RN/PR)

◀16

17▲

18▲ 19▼

▲20 ▼21

20. Submarines maintain many of the traditions of the surface navy, including the need to wear the paying-off pennant when entering harbours for the last time before refit. The length of the paying-off pennant corresponds to the length of service during the commission. This is *Conqueror* arriving at Portsmouth. (Mike Lennon)

21. Early experience with the *Valiant*s showed that in order to dive deeper, the SSNs of the future would need to have fewer openings in the pressure hull; thus, when the *Swiftsure* Class was ordered in 1967, the number of torpedo tubes was cut to five and the boat's hull-form changed. The six *Swiftsure*s are slightly shorter than the *Valiant*s yet have a more streamlined appearance above the water. This impression seems to be generated by the smaller fin, the positioning of the forward diving/control planes and the new rudder profile. (RN/HMS *Neptune*)

22. Escorted by *Labrador*, her nuclear safety boat, *Swiftsure* leaves a wintry Faslane. The Type 1006 radar aerial has been raised, as well as the HF direction-finding aerial. On the bridge, the White Ensign is worn on a removable staff and the commissioning pennant on a whip aerial. This boat was commissioned in 1973 and, like all six members of the class, was built at Barrow-in-Furness by Vickers Shipbuilding. (RN/HMS *Neptune*)

23. The Irish Sea provides the venue for this view of *Swiftsure* underway on the surface, with search periscope and radio mast very much in evidence. The *Swiftsure*s are capable of over 30kts when dived and can reach a depth of about 3,000ft. Besides the regular heavyweight torpedoes like Tigerfish and Mk 8, SSNs can also be armed with the Sub-Harpoon anti-ship missile. Every British submarine, and presumably those of France, the USA and the USSR, is always prepared for operational duties and carries food, spares and full armament at all times. (RN/HMS *Neptune*)

22 ▲   23 ▼

▲24

24. *Sovereign*, the second of the *Swiftsure* Class to be completed by Vickers, achieved major feats of navigation and seamanship when in 1976 (two years after first commissioning) she surfaced through the ice at the North Pole. The Arctic Ocean is now thought to be a major operational area for nuclear-powered submarines and several have carried out visits to the Pole in recent years. (RN/HMS *Neptune*)

25. Known to the Fleet as 'Super B', the third member of the *Swiftsure* Class to be commissioned was *Superb*. During the early days of the Falklands crisis, it was thought that she was operating in the South Atlantic, but it has since emerged that her radio call-sign was used by *Endurance* off South Georgia in order to confuse Argentine Naval Intelligence; at the time, *Superb* was under refit. (RN/HMS *Neptune*)

▼25

26▲

26. Off the coast of Ayrshire, *Superb* demonstrates the close contact between the Fleet Air Arm and the Submarine Service. At the time this photograph was taken the *Superb* was the latest British submarine and the Sea King HAS 2 the most advanced anti-submarine helicopter in the world. Both have now been surpassed by other types yet remain operationally effective (RN/HMS *Neptune*)

27. The end of another patrol and *Spartan* slides into Plymouth Sound, en route on the naval base which is also home to the Second Submarine Squadron. SM 2 has *Swiftsure*, *Trafalgar* and conventional diesel-electric submarines under command. *Spartan* was commissioned in September 1979 and is seen here rigged for entering harbour, complete even with the jackstaff on the bow. (RN/HMS *Drake*)

27▼

▲28

28. The last of the *Swiftsure* Class was *Splendid*, launched in November 1977 and commissioned in March 1981. She cost about £97 million (as compared to *Dreadnought*'s £18.5 million in 1963) and has an average annual running cost of nearly £4 million. Nevertheless, the British SSNs are some of the most important and valuable naval assets to the NATO alliance. *Splendid* is pictured leaving Faslane with her search periscope (topped with an electronic counter-measures housing), radar and radio masts raised. (RN)

29. Always seeking to improve on the design and construction of its submarines, the Royal Navy requested a further class of SSNs to follow the *Swiftsure*s. The *Trafalgar* Class, which will comprise at least eight boats, was announced in 1977, when the first of the class was ordered from Vickers. Shown here on builder's sea trials in 1982, *Trafalgar* is outwardly similar to the *Swiftsure*s. (Vickers)

30. Once under the White Ensign, *Trafalgar* was put through her paces during an extensive work-up period before being declared operational in 1983. The class has been designed to be quieter than previous submarines and to this extent some careful work in terms of space rearrangement and machinery mounting has been done. Like other SSNs, the boats will be used to search out and destroy enemy submarines and, as a secondary role, high-value surface vessels in the event of war. (Vickers)

31. *Trafalgar* (foreground) and *Turbulent* are fitted out at Barrow. *Trafalgar* has just had her diesel exhaust (back) and snort induction masts fitted; *Turbulent* is still being worked on and her fin and bridge are covered to allow all-weather completion. Nuclear-powered submarines have small diesel generators to provide auxiliary (and emergency) electric power. (Vickers)

32. During her first operational cruise *Turbulent* visited Liverpool (near her adopted town of Warrington), and she is pictured here alongside a wharf in the commercial harbour. Auxiliary power is being provided by the diesel generator, and the search periscope has yet to be lowered after its use for the passage up the River Mersey. (RN/CPO Drew/FOSM)

33. The launching of another SSN: this is *Tireless*, the third of the *Trafalgar*s, which commissioned in late 1985. It is possible that these boats will replace the early *Valiant*s in RN service and that a sixth class will be ordered in 1988 to replace the Improved *Valiant*s and early *Swiftsure*s, but much will depend on the Trident submarine programme. (RN)

◀31

32▲ 33▼

▲ 34   ▼ 35

34. The first test for the Royal Navy's nuclear-powered attack submarines came in 1982 when the Argentines invaded the Falkland Islands. For the RN, the speedy despatch of at least two SSNs was an immediate measure, and the very fact that they were known by the Argentine Navy to be in the area must have contributed to the absence of surface ship activity by the invaders. Most attention has, of course, focused on *Conqueror* and her action which resulted in the sinking of the Argentine cruiser *General Belgrano*; she is pictured here returning to Faslane. (RN)

35. The battered paint-work and the 'Jolly Roger' pennant bear witness to the work done by *Conqueror* in the South Atlantic, which included covert operations with special forces. The boat's skipper, Commander Christopher Wreford-Brown, was awarded the Distinguished Service Order for his part in the campaign. Other members of the crew were also decorated. (RN)

36. Moving out into the Atlantic, the French SSBN *L'Inflexible* shows off her large fin-mounted diving/control plane and, immediately aft of the fin, the emergency escape hatch for underwater recovery. The large doors, marked with the numbers 1 to 16, are the lifting hatches for the M-4 missiles. (DCN)

36▶

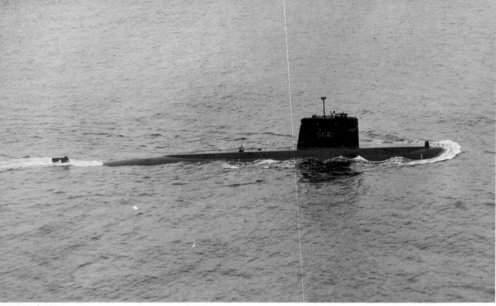

37

37. The French nuclear-powered submarine *Rubis* underway on the surface off the Atlantic coast of France. Though having a slightly similar profile to British SSNs, the SNA-72 class are almost 50ft shorter. The French Navy is scheduled to continue its SSN programme with another class for the 1990s and the next century. (*Marine Nationale*)

38, 39. With the aid of commercial tugs, the quietest nuclear-powered submarine in NATO, *Turbulent*, enters the lock system at Liverpool prior to her first 'public' port visit. The British SSN programme is continuing despite the possible shortage of manpower and resources as the emphasis switches to the Trident programme. (RN/CPO Drew)

40. The first official artist's impression of the Trident Class of nuclear-powered missile-carrying submarine which is destined to maintain the British independent nuclear deterrent into the next century. The Trident missile has a range of over 6,000nm, and each of the sixteen carried would have thirteen multiple independently targeted re-entry vehicle (MIRV) warheads. (RN)

▼38

41. The first US Trident missile submarine, *Ohio* (SSBN-726), pictured underway on the surface (not her normal environment) during a preliminary cruise in 1982. The submarine is now part of the active Pacific Fleet, armed with twenty-four Trident 1C4 ballistic missiles and about eight Mk 68 heavy-weight torpedoes.

42. The Royal Navy now keeps a submarine in the South Atlantic more regularly than prior to 1982. The first boat to go down after the cessation of hostilities was *Warspite*; she returned to Faslane in March 1983 and was met by the UK Secretary of State for Defence, Michael Hesletine. (RN)

43. The Royal Navy now keeps a repair ship on the South Atlantic station, operating from San Carlos Water, enabling submarines not only to receive assistance for repairs, but also collect the mail and stores. *Bar Protector* is one of a number of ships taken up from trade and one of several to act as forward support ships. The ship is photographed (with *Warspite* alongside) on her second South Atlantic deployment. (RN/FOSM)

41

42▲   43▼

▲44

▼45

44. In 1984 the Royal Navy purchased the former *Stena Seaspread* to act as the San Carlos forward repair ship, and she is operated by the Royal Fleet Auxiliary in this role. This view, taken from a naval helicopter, shows *Valiant* alongside RFA *Diligence* (as *Stena Seaspread* is now called). A rest and recreation visit to this vessel might well be the only surface contact made by a submarine – except that at Gibraltar – during more than 100 days on patrol. (RN/FOSM)

45. Modern submarine weapons now include submarine-launched guided missiles like the McDonnell Douglas Sub-Harpoon, photographed here during a test firing from *Churchill* during 1981. The missile is designed to surface-skim towards a high-value target such as an enemy aircraft carrier or other large warship, and several are carried aboard most submarines in addition to the more traditional torpedoes. (McDonnell Douglas)

46. The 21in (53cm) heavyweight torpedo is still the standard submarine weapon, either wire-guided against submarine targets and some surface ships, or free running against surface targets. This drill-type heavyweight torpedo is being loaded aboard a *Swiftsure* Class SSN from the torpedo recovery ship RMAS *Toreador* at Faslane. The torpedoes pass through the open hatch and via a system of internal hatches and pulleys into the Torpedo Room some two decks below. (RN)

47. The effect of a modern heavyweight torpedo can be judged from this photograph, which was taken through *Splendid*'s periscope during air-launched missile trials against the former guided missile destroyer *Devonshire*. After the strike amidships by a Sea Eagle missile, *Splendid* fired a Tigerfish Mk 24 Mod 0 torpedo, causing crippling damage to the stern. (RN)

▲48　▼49

48. The nuclear-powered sub-marine does not often come to periscope depth, for to do so would be to create a target visible to surveillance systems, including, it is presumed, the various 'spy' satellites now in service. Here the advanced Barr & Stroud search periscope of *Turbulent* provides the boat's captain, Cdr. Tim Lightoller, with a view of the Irish Sea shipping during a passage southwards from Faslane. (Author)

49. The controls of the modern SSN bear a close resemblance to those of modern aircraft, except that there is no view ahead. The US Navy uses a system of artificially generated graphics, but the Royal Navy relies on standard instrumentation. In this photograph taken aboard a *Swiftsure* Class submarine, the depth gauge is masked off with tape for security reasons. (RN/HMS *Neptune*)

50. One of the most important jobs in the boat's control room is keeping the 'plot' – the navi-gational chart which informs the navigator and officer of the watch of the submarine's posi-tion. In modern nuclear-powered submarines such as *Turbulent* the raw data is pro-vided from several sources, including the SINS (Submarine Inertial Navigation System), SNAPS (Ship's Navigation Automatic Plotting System) and the newly developed KDU (Keyboard Display Unit). (Author)

51. In *Turbulent* these systems have their own names – Sammy the SINS (hidden behind the Leading Hand on the right), Danny the Decca Navigator (above the Petty Officer's head), Sally the SNAPS (under the chart table) and Kenneth the KDU (under the PO's hand). (Author)

52. The business end of the SSN is the Weapons Storage Compartment, the former Forward Torpedo Room; the latter term is now out of use because the compartment is the only one provided for weapons and because the torpedo has been supplemented by the submarine-launched missile in modern Royal Navy boats. This view shows a *Valiant* Class boat: of the six tubes, No 4 open is to receive a reload torpedo, missile or mine. (RN/HMS *Dolphin*)

53. Accommodation, even on the three-deck SSN, is limited. This is the wardroom of *Turbulent*, showing the dining table and, behind, two cabins in which three of the boat's senior officers share space. The captain is the only officer with his own cabin, and that is positioned within a few paces of the control room. (Author)

54. The Senior Ratings share accommodation twenty to a messdeck, whilst the 55 or so Junior Ratings of a modern SSN have a much more confined space. There is, however, room for the television/video recorder and the hi-fi, plus a table to eat from, work on and relax around. (Author)

55. The Weapons Storage space is also used for trials work and when visitors are aboard, the lower storage rails converting into makeshift bunks. On the deck can be seen three months' supply of video and movie film for the crew's off-duty entertainment. (Author)

▲52   ▼53

54▲ 55▼

▲56 ▼57

56. In February 1963 it was announced by the British Government that the independent nuclear deterrent of the United Kingdom would from the 1968 be the charge of the Royal Navy, carried in a class of five nuclear-powered ballistic missile-carrying submarines (SSBNs). Four of the five boats commissioned between 1967 and 1969; the fifth was cancelled after a change of government in 1965. Four SSBNs represent the bare minimum necessary to keep one at sea at all times. This the first of the class, *Resolution*, leaving its home base of Faslane. Note that the search radar and search periscope masts have been raised. (RN)

57. *Resolution* was commissioned in October 1967 after commencing sea trials in June of that year. Like so many modern British submarines, she was built by Vickers at Barrow. In this view of a Sea King helicopter transferring a member of the ship's company during a work-up after refit, the sixteen Polaris missile bay hatches can be seen aft of the fin. Also visible are the rudder, the forward control planes and the diesel exhaust on the fin top. (RN)

58. In the early 1980s the British Polaris missiles, which had been purchased from the United States, were modernised in the United Kingdom under the 'Chevaline' programme. *Revenge*, pictured here in the River Clyde, was the first of the four 'R-boats' to receive the updated missiles, which each have three 60kT nuclear warheads capable of tracking independently and re-entering the Earth's atmosphere separately, thus enabling more than one target to be selected. (RN/HMS *Neptune*)

59. Although normally stationed at Faslane, the Clyde Submarine Base, and operating far away on submerged patrols known only to a handful of senior RN personnel, the Polaris submarines do from time to time visit other naval ports. Here *Repulse* is entering Portsmouth Harbour in the mid-1970s, with the crew lined up on the forward casing in Procedure Alpha. (Mike Lennon)

60. Moving up the Forth to Rosyth, *Repulse* flies her paying-off pennant prior to commencing a refit at the base. For a nuclear-powered submarine, the refit cycle includes a two-year period alongside for modernisation and nuclear-reactor work, including the periodic replacement of the fuel cells. All work on SSBNs is secret, thus maintaining the credibility of the deterrent force. (RN/FOSNI)

58▲

59▲ 60▼

▲61 ▼62

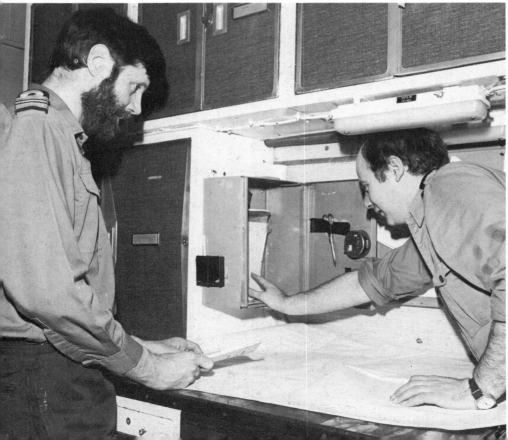

61. Life aboard an SSBN is a little more comfortable than aboard a conventional submarine or even a modern SSN. This is the commanding officer of *Renown*'s port crew (there are two crews for each SSBN), Cdr Mike Gregory, at the search periscope. The boat also has an attack periscope and is armed to carry at least six Type 24 Tigerfish or similar ASW and anti-ship torpedoes. These weapons are probably for self-defence. (RN)

62. The Polaris missile firing authentication codes are kept in two safes on board the SSBN, one inside the other. Only two officers know the combination of each safe. In this photograph of *Renown*, the Weapons Electrical Officer and the First Lieutenant are seen removing the codes during an exercise. Note the light action dress of both officers. (RN)

63. The working conditions aboard an R-boat are relatively clean and comfortable, especially compared to those aboard a conventional submarine. This is the Polaris Missile Compartment, and the ratings in this view are carrying out a series of checks on the system. To the right is the inspection hatch for the No 3 missile tube. (RN)

64. Tests are also carried out in the Missile Control Compartment, and in this view, again taken aboard *Renown*, the Weapons Electrical Officer is seen with his left hand holding the firing trigger which, if the correct sequence were to be followed, would allow a Polaris missile to be launched. The 'readiness' of the missiles is periodically tested but safeguards are built in to the system to prevent any likelihood of a mishap. (RN)

65. In the actual event, the launch of a Polaris missile would appear like this to anyone within sight, but for the crew of an SSBN there would merely be the noise of compressed air filling the missile compartment and some vibration as the missile left the submarine. There would be no shouted orders of 'Fire!', only quiet, calm procedures practised many times before. (RN)

66, 67. Even aboard a submarine as large as *Renown* living space is at a premium. Photograph 66 shows the bunk and locker space in Junior Ratings' sleeping area, whilst 67 shows the largest compartment in the boat, the Junior Ratings' dining hall. This compartment is also used as cinema and entertainments hall.

◀65

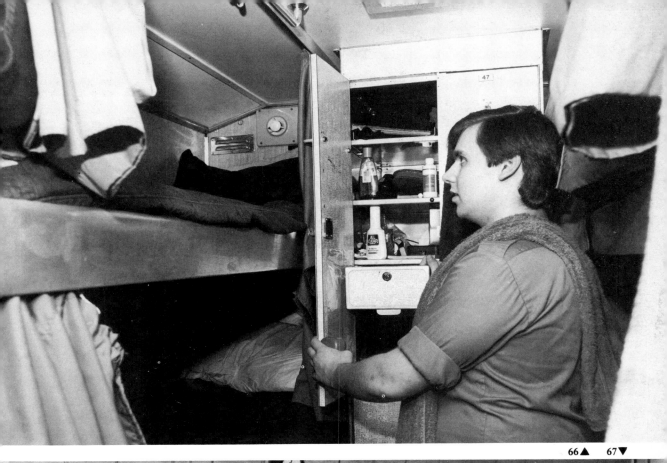

▲68   ▼69

68. When off duty, the Junior Ratings have a recreation space for the playing of traditional 'uckers' (the Royal Navy's ludo) and, as shown here, young ladies also brighten up the environment. (RN)

69. Even for the boat's officers, accommodation space is small and, unusually for modern warships, cabin space has to be shared. Here *Renown's* Supply Officer, Lt. Rowland Nurick, works on 'packs' in a compartment which he shares with four other junior officers.

70. *Renown's* wardroom is simple and well designed, with barely space enough for the normal trappings of service meals, yet even the boat's trophies are taken to sea. Note the working rig of shirts and sandals adopted by the officers, seen here taking lunch. (RN)

71. Apart from looking after the missiles, there is other important work to be carried out aboard an SSBN. For example, considerable care is taken to make sure that the boat's environment is in accordance with specially prescribed standards: constant checks are made by the health physics staff for possible radiation, and, as shown in this photograph, the self-defence torpedo tubes are regularly checked for performance in the Torpedo Stowage Area. (RN)

72. With a continuous throughput of personnel, even aboard the 'R-boats', the Royal Navy is always careful to ensure absolute safety. In this photograph, a trainee is given instruction in the emergency escape procedure at the forward escape tower. He is wearing a survival suit to protect him from the harsh underwater conditions. (RN)

73. It is vital that the commander of a Polaris submarine is aware of the exact launch position of a missile if it is to fall precisely on target (which could be a land-based missile silo, to prevent a second wave of ballistic missiles being launched.) In British SSBNs the navigation centre, off the main control room, houses the SINS (Submarine Inertial Navigation System) and several other navigation systems. (RN)

74. The new Trident missile facility at the Bangor (Maine) Naval Submarine Base has a Magnetic Silencing Facility, where *Ohio* was pictured alongside in August 1982. (USN/Linda Skonieczny)

75. The third generation of SSNs for the Soviet Navy was the successful 'Victor-I' type, built from 1965 to 1974 as anti-submarine and anti-ship submarines. The design includes the 'Albacore' hull shape and a new type of nuclear reactor, giving the vessels at least 32kts underwater. The main armament is six torpedo tubes, all forward, and the boats can launch encapsulated missiles if necessary. At present, NATO sources indicate that the class is deployed with the Northern Red Banner Fleet, based in the White Sea. (NATO)

76. (Overleaf) Going . . . going . . . gone! The launching of any vessel is an important occasion and so often the Americans commit their latest naval vessels to the water on a Saturday, to allow for full public representation. Launching ceremonies also attract the 'top brass', in this case from Washington DC and the nearby Headquarters of the Atlantic Fleet. (Newport News SB & DD)

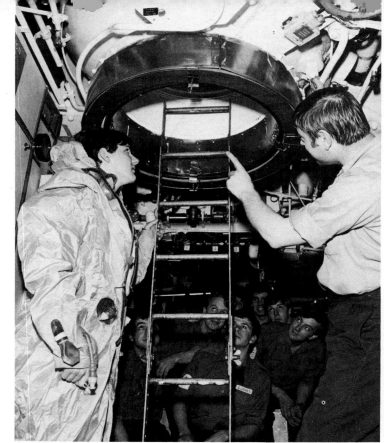

▲72   ▼73

▲77 ▼78

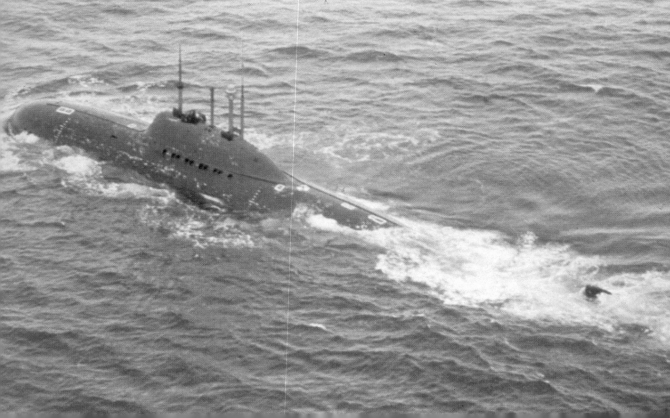

79▲

77. In the Soviet Navy, the original 'Victor-Is' were followed from 1972 by the uprated and modified 'Victor-II' Class, which are slightly longer but retain the same successful hull form. 'Victor IIs' can carry the encapsulated anti-submarine missile known to NATO as SS-N-15, as well as mines and other submarine devices. (NATO)

78. The latest class of Soviet-built nuclear-powered attack submarine is the 'Alpha', which caused quite a stir in NATO circles in the early 1970s because of its reported 42kts dived speed and its ability to dive to at least 3,000ft. The 'Alpha' – spelt 'Alfa' by the USN – is the product of intense research by the Soviet Union and has resulted in a new hull design, with new construction materials and a new reactor system. The standard armament is the wire-guided torpedo for anti-submarine and anti-surface-ship roles. (NATO)

79. *Nautilus* was the world's first nuclear-powered submarine, the boat making its historic signal 'Underway on nuclear power' on 17 January 1955; three years later, she made a transit under the North Pole en route from the Pacific Fleet base at Pearl Harbor, Hawaii, to Portland naval base in southern England. The boat was decommissioned in 1980 to stand in Washington Navy Yard as a memorial to early SSN work, but a decision was later made to transfer her to Groton, New England, where she was built. (USN)

80. *Skipjack* (SSN-585) and her five sister-boats were the first US nuclear submarines to be built to the now familiar 'teardrop' hull design for fast submerged speeds and better noise reduction. She was the first US submarine with a single propeller and when commissioned in April 1959 was also the world's fastest, capable of more than 30kts dived. In 1985 the four remaining *Skipjack* Class boats were still active in the US Navy, *Scorpion* having been lost with all hands in 1968. (USN)

80▼

▲81

81. In 1957 the US Navy decided to continue its nuclear-powered submarine programme with the *Thresher* Class of 4,300-ton (dived) boats capable of higher surfaced speed than the *Skipjack*s and of deeper operations. *Thresher* herself (SSN-593) was lost in 1963, and the lead-boat of the class is now *Permit* (SSN-594), which commissioned on May 29 1962 and joined the Pacific Fleet. She is pictured here in San Francisco Bay. (USN)

82. Built at the Portsmouth (USA) naval shipyard, *Tinosa* (SSN-606) is another *Thresher* Class SSN and, like her thirteen sister-boats, she carries the SUBROC anti-submarine system, four torpedo tubes amidships and (probably) Sub-Harpoon. She is seen here off Portsmouth in 1979. (Mike Lennon)

83. In the ten years from 1967 the US Navy commissioned 37 new *Sturgeon* Class attack submarines, each with a displacement of nearly 5,000 tons and an underwater speed of at least 35kts. The first of the class was *Sturgeon* (SSN-637) herself, built by the Electric Boat Division of General Dynamics in New England. To improve the boats' performance at periscope depth, the diving planes are lower on the fin as compared to earlier SSNs. (USN)

▼82

▲84

84. *Whale* (SSN-638), the second of the *Sturgeon* Class, was also built by the Quincy Division of General Dynamics and commissioned in 1968. Like many of the US Navy's nuclear-powered submarines she occasionally visits foreign waters: in this photograph she is seen at Portsmouth, November 1982. The boat is under tow, with *Excellent*, the RN shore establishment, in the background. This view gives a good idea of the difference in size between the attack periscope and the larger search periscope. (Mike Lennon)

85. Some of the American nuclear-powered submarines are very aptly named: this is *Hammerhead* (SSN-663), shown arriving at Portsmouth with nearly all her officers, plus a British submariner for liaison duties, on the fin top. As the bow section of this class of submarine is taken up with a large active sonar, the torpedo tubes are situated amidships. (Mike Lennon)

▼85

86. When *Lapon* (SSN-661) visited the Solent in 1979, she was photographed with several masts raised, including what appears to be the diesel induction system, with perhaps a form of electronic countermeasures on top. The appearance of US Navy nuclear submarines is characterized by fin-mounted diving planes and a long hull area aft of the fin (or 'sail' in US parlance). (Mike Lennon)

87. Dressed overall, *Billfish* (SSN-676), an Electric Boat-built SSN, was present at the Silver Jubilee Review at Spithead in 1977. The boat had been commissioned some six years earlier and was part of the Atlantic Fleet. Note the hand-grabs on the diving planes; the latter often act as additional standing positions for such occasions as naval reviews. (Mike Lennon)

87 ▼

▲88

88. This aerial view of *Batfish* (SSN-681) taken shortly before she was commissioned into the US Navy, shows the submarine's after hull and the transducers for the specialized sonar used for patrols under and close to the Arctic ice pack. The *Sturgeon* Class were the first boats with single screws to surface at the North Pole. (USN)

89. The conventional submarine has always been considered, until recently at least, the quietest of all underwater vessels, even though the SSN can remain submerged for longer periods. The problem with the SSN is that its nuclear reactor and associated turbines have inherent noise-generating components. As long ago as 1964 the US Navy began work on quietening its modern submarines, and *Glenard P. Lipscomb* (SSN-685) was built as a nuclear-powered Turbo-Electric Drive Submarine (TEDS). Although many of the design features went into the *Los Angeles* Class, TEDS were not proceeded with further. (Mike Lennon)

90. In 1970 the US Government authorized the first constructions in the new *Los Angeles* Class attack submarines, and since then it has been progressively announced that more than sixty such boats will be procured. The first, *Los Angeles* (SSN-688) herself, built by Newport News Shipbuilding and incorporating special features designed to lessen noise, was commissioned in 1976. The class will continue in production until about 1990. (USN)

91. *Los Angeles* is capable of at least 35kts underwater and can dive to about 1,500ft. Her armament is the standard 21in/53cm heavyweight torpedo, using four tubes amidships which can also take the Sub-Harpoon encapsulated missile, as well as the planned Tomahawk cruise-missile; twelve of the latter will be carried by the first units of the class. (Newport News SB & DD)

▼89

90▲   91▼

92. On sea trials from the builder's yards in Virginia, *Baton Rouge* (SSN-689), the second of the *Los Angeles* Class, cuts a powerful swathe through the ocean. These boats cost about $225 million each, but the price rises as more complex systems, such as satellite communications, torpedo fire control and advanced sonars, are fitted. (Newport News SB & DD/Lloyd Everton)

93. *Cincinnati* (SSN-693) was the sixth boat of the *Los Angeles* Class to be commissioned and is seen here on builder's sea trials in April 1978. These boats are reported to be very quiet compared to earlier classes, and have the ability to take at least two submarine targets simultaneously. This view gives a good indication of the fin-top arrangement, with cockpit-like compartments for the officers of the watch and other watchkeepers during surface running. (Newport News SB & DD)

94. A dramatic view of a nuclear-powered submarine breaking the surface during emergency trials. This is *Birmingham* (SSN-695), the fifth unit of the *Los Angeles* Class to have been built in Virginia by Newport News Shipbuilding. The bow section does not hold torpedo tubes but, within the outer casing, encloses an array of sonar antennas for long-range target acquisition. (Newport News SB & DD)

95. In 1973 the US Navy issued a series of photographs showing the internal compartments of its latest SSNs. This view of the control room of *Archerfish* (SSN-678), one of the *Sturgeon* Class boats, shows crew members (the planesmen) 'flying' the submarine through the Electric Boat Company's test range in Long Island Sound. (USN)

96. This view of the control room of *Whale* (SSN-638) shows that, even between sister-boats, the design of internal compartments varies as in-service modifications are taken up by later units. According to the official USN caption, the crewman with his back to the camera is standing by the ballast control panel during a submerged passage. (USN/PHC Andersen)

97. During trials in the Pacific Ocean, *Los Angeles* (SSN-688), the first of the new generation of nuclear-powered attack submarines, was put through a series of demanding exercises. After each one, every system was thoroughly checked. In this view, two of the weapons team inspect one of the four 21in torpedo tubes, which are situated amidships in most USN boats. (USN)

▲95   ▼96

97▶

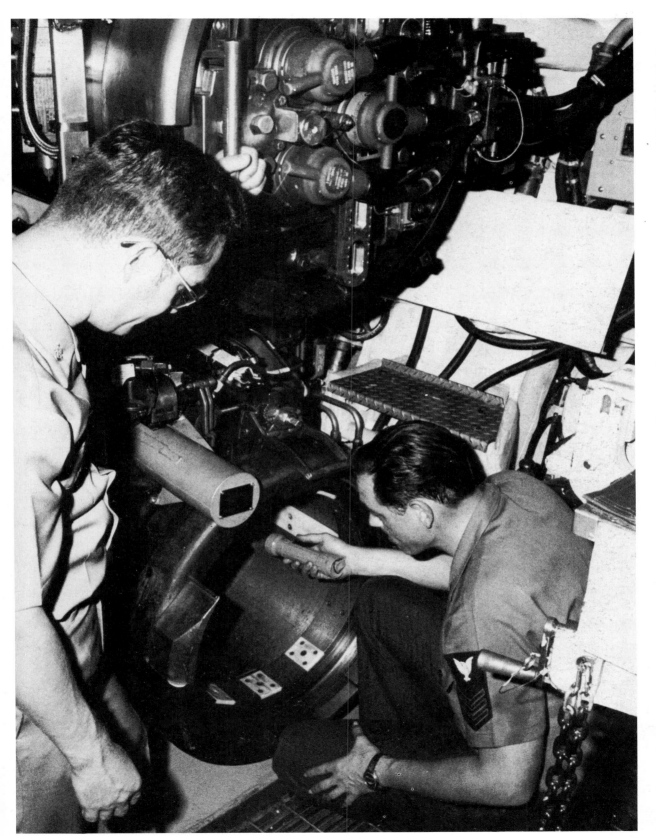

▲98

98. The loss of two nuclear-powered submarines within five years led the US Navy to build Deep Submergence Rescue Vehicles, and this is one of the nuclear-powered vessels. They are air transportable, and in this photograph DSRV-HTV (Hull Test Vehicle) is being loaded aboard a USAF C-141A Starlifter and would be available for world-wide transportation and deployment if required. (Lockheed)

99. Although commissioned in the early 1960s, the *Ethan Allan* Class of SSBNs (*John Marshall*, SSN-611, is pictured here in 1962) were converted in 1980–81 to SSNs. The US Navy authorized the 'decommissioning' of the tubes which had been designed for Polaris A-2 and A-3 missiles, and the space was filled with concrete to act as ballast, thus ensuring accurate trim when diving. Four *Ethan Allans* and three *George Washingtons* were re-classified as training SSNs, one of each class being held in reserve for the Pacific Fleet. (USN)

100. Photographed off the coast of the Eastern United States, *Lafayette* (SSBN-616) was, when commissioned in April 1963, the largest submarine built in the Western World. Although not as quiet as the later *Benjamin Franklin* Class, the *Lafayette*s have been useful platforms for both Polaris and Poseidon SLBMs. Craft of this type have a submerged speed of 30kts plus, but on patrol they would rarely move that fast because of the self-generated noise and other disturbances which could give their position away. (USN/PH2 Bayse)

101. *Benjamin Franklin* (SSBN-640), built by Electric Boat, was commissioned in October 1965 as a Polaris/Poseidon carrier, but in 1979–81 she was, with several others of her class, taken out of service for conversion to operate Trident missiles. The work was carried out at the Portsmouth (US) naval shipyard, and the boat was subsequently based at King's Bay, Georgia, the East Coast home of the Trident Fleet. (USN)

▼99

102. The modern power of the American nuclear deterrent force is the Trident missile: an example is seen here immediately after launch from *John C. Calhoun* (SSBN-630) off the east coast of Florida. The Trident 1C4 missile of the converted *Benjamin Franklin* Class submarines has a range of about 4,350nm and has been replaced by the Trident 2D5 missile (which is also to be procured for the Royal Navy). (USAF)

103. The first successful nuclear ballistic missile for use in submarines was Polaris, which was supplied both to the US Navy and to the RN. The first modification programme produced the A-2 version: one is seen here being surface-launched from *Henry Clay* (SSBN-625) off Cape Canaveral, Florida. Note the telemetry mast on the fin and the launch ejection of shields and casings. For a surface launch the submarine is heeled to port when a starboard tube is used, and *vice versa*. (USN)

104. After the Polaris programme came the Poseidon missile, a two-stage system which entered service in about 1970 (aboard *James Madison*, SSBN-627) and which is destined to remain active until 1990, when the *Ohio* Class will be fully operational with Trident. This photograph was taken during the boat's first shakedown cruise with a Poseidon warload; again, the telemetry mast is clearly visible. (USN)

105. Because the Trident missile is larger than its two main predecessors, the design of a new class of submarine to carry the Trident 2 was authorized in 1974. Each boat named after an American state, the *Ohio* Class has good noise reduction systems, good habitability and crew accommodation and sufficient room for 'growth', in order to take the future-generation Trident 3 missile in the late 1990s and the twenty-first century. This is *Michigan* (SSBN-727), the second of the class. (General Dynamics)

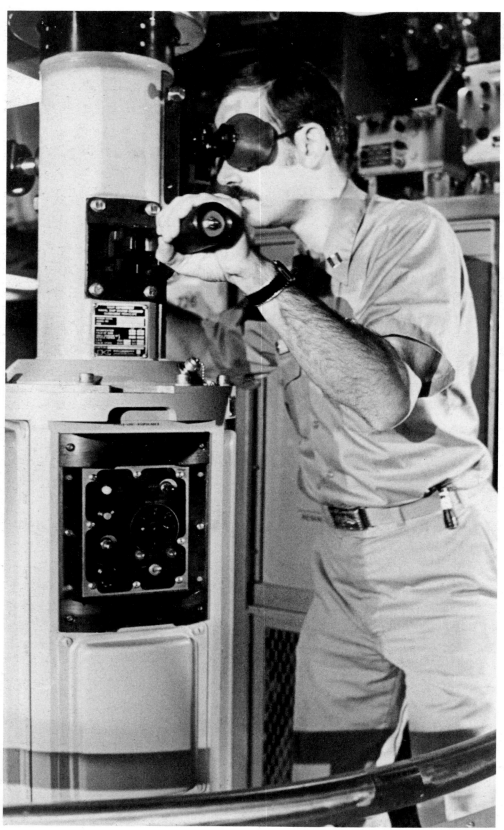

106. During a pre-commissioning shake-down cruise for *Ohio* (SSBN-726), the first of the US Navy's purpose-built Trident missile submarines, all the systems were checked. Here, a lieutenant USN uses the attack periscope to obtain a surface fix, although on an operational patrol the highly accurate SINS (Submarine Inertial Navigation System) would be used to chart the submarine's progress across the oceans of the world. (USN/PH1 Anderson)

107. Although the primary weapon system of the *Ohio* Class is the Trident SLBM, the boats have been designed for the carriage of heavyweight anti-submarine torpedoes in tubes slightly forward of amidships. The torpedoes carried, and illustrated here, are the Mk 68, and four tubes (and as many reloads) are available. (USN/PH1 Anderson)

108. During a 'battle stations' drill aboard *Ohio*, the control board in the missile control centre is fully manned and the status of each of the twenty-four Trident missile tubes is given on the panel in front of the Chief Missile Technician. The *Ohio* Class have been armed initially with the Trident 1C4, but the boats will be re-fitted with Trident 2D5 in the mid-1990s. (USN)

◄106

107▲   108▼

▲109 ▼110

111▲

109. The first class of Soviet-built nuclear-powered attack submarines appeared in 1958 and were named 'November' by NATO. With a dived displacement of 5,000 tons and an underwater speed of about 30kts, the class was designed with a long hull shape. According to NATO submariners, the boats are noisy underwater, and the twelve or so still in commission are probably used for training and trials. (Via *Navy International*)

110. This 'November' Class SSN was caught on the surface in the North Atlantic by the crew of a Royal Air Force Nimrod reconnaissance aircraft; it is believed that the submarine had suffered a series of malfunctions in its life support systems and had made an emergency surface. Note the crew members on deck and the sonar array forward of the bow planes.

111. In April 1979 this 'November' Class submarine was spotted on the surface and, unusually, wearing a pennant number. Even so, it is not possible to give a name to the boat because the Soviet Red Banner Fleet does not allocate pennant numbers to its hulls, rather using them as fleet or squadron numbers which are periodically changed and re-allocated as a vessel changes geographical location.

112. The Soviet Navy is the only maritime force actively to pursue a policy of building cruise-missile carrying submarines, and the first design, built in the 1960s was the 'Juliett', a conventionally powered craft. Those remaining in commission appear to be stationed in the Baltic Sea. Note the extended 'Snoop Slab' navigational and search radar antenna and the blast holes in the outer casing for missile launch.

112▼

◄113

114▲

113. The 'Echo' Class was originally envisaged as a cruise-missile carrying series of submarines, but between 1969 and 1974 the first group were converted to SSN standard. The hull shape is basically the same as the earlier 'Novembers' but the fin is more reminiscent of Soviet conventional boats. The vessels have stern and bow torpedo tubes, the latter necessitating the positioning of the active sonar above the forward casing in a characteristic 'horn' stub antenna. The 'Echo-I' photographed here has its radio mast erected (which, it seems, is stowed in the outer casing rather than retracted as in NATO SSNs). (Via *Navy International*)

114. Photographs of Soviet submarines are very difficult to come by, especially of those which are nuclear-powered and which do not need to surface for air. Occasionally, NATO or other friendly reconnaissance aircraft catch them on the surface, perhaps in some form of temporary disablement. This is the latest Soviet SSN, one of the 'Alpha' Class. (NATO)

115. The Soviet Navy entered the ballistic missile carrying 'club' in 1958 when construction of the first 'Golf' Class submarine was commenced. The class has a characteristically large fin with three vertical launch tubes for intercontinental nuclear ballistic missiles. Many boats are now out of commission and only the later, modified vessels remain in service, some in the Pacific Ocean. The 'Golf' Class vessels have a dived speed of 14kts and a range of about 23,000nm on their diesel-electric power system. (NATO)

115▼

◀116

117▲

116. The 'Hotel' Class was the first of the Russian SSBNs, using the same fin design as the earlier 'Golf' to carry vertical launch tubes. This 'Hotel-II' Class boat was photographed by a Nimrod long-range patrol aircraft in the North Atlantic in 1972.

117. A 'Hotel-II' Class SSBN, capable of carrying six SS-N-8 SLBMs, photographed off the coast of the United States, demonstrating that Soviet SSBNs are deployed far afield – perhaps further than is necessary for the self-defence of the USSR. (NATO)

118. Only carrying twelve SLBMs, the 'Delta' Class was first identified in 1972 as another generation of Soviet missile-carrying submarine. The 'Delta-I' group (of which this boat, photographed in 1976, is one of eighteen known to have been built in 1972–77) later gave way to -II and -III batches which can carry 16 SS-N-8 and SS-N-18 SLBMs respectively. All three 'Delta' groups have the easily identifiable missile housing in the after casing, giving the submarines a 'humped' appearance when on the surface.

118▼

▲119

119. Characterized by its enlarged missile tube 'hump', the 'Delta-III' class SSBNs were first seen in 1976, and it is thought that fifteen have now been commissioned into Red Banner Fleet service. The SS-N-18 missiles carried by this group each have a range of over 4,000nm. The boats have a submerged speed of 24kts and carry eighteen torpedoes for six tubes as a self-defence measure. (NATO)

120. In about 1980 the NATO powers became aware that the Soviet Navy was about to launch the largest submarine ever built – a boat with a submerged displacement of about 30,000 tons, powered by two nuclear reactors and carrying twenty of a new type of SLBM. The first of the class was launched in 1980 and christened 'Typhoon' by NATO. The missile tubes are mounted forward of the fin and the hull shape is thought to be a catamaran. The SS-N-X missiles thought to be carried each have nine warheads, and each missile is capable of striking NATO targets from almost any ocean in the world. This picture was taken of a sea trial in 1982; by 1985, two boats of the class were thought to be operational.

▼120